ME ROBOTS

Mechanical Engineering Basics

Level 1 Training Manual · Training Version

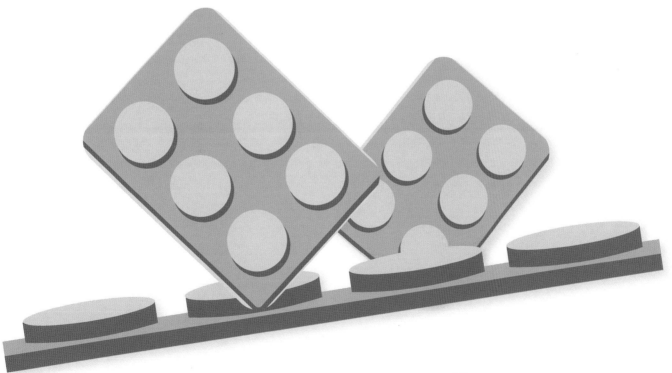

St. Catherine
University

WELCOME

Dear ME Robots Instructor,

On behalf of St. Catherine University and the *ME Robots: Mechanical Engineering Basics* program, thank you for training with us.

The *ME Robots Curriculum* is divided into three levels. Each requires 4 lessons in order to prepare students to achieve a challenge project. As you learned in training, you can present these lessons in several possible venues: as an after-school program, as a day camp, as a series of weekend programs, etc.

This booklet was created to supplement your training workshop with us. It reminds you of essential concepts and provides some preparation guidelines. However, it does assume that you have already done the training. Feel free to make notes in the booklet for your future reference. We appreciate your feed-back on how to improve this in the future.

Welcome to the exciting world of Robotics and Mechanical Engineering! We hope you have fun.

Sincerely,

Sherri Kreuser

Yvonne Ng

© 2008 St. Catherine University

Mechanical Engineering Basics

Level 1 Training Manual • Training Version

St. Catherine University would like to acknowledge the following foundations for their generous support of the ME Robots program:

**Hugh J. Andersen
Foundation**

Children's **Foundation**

Thrivent Financial for Lutherans·
Foundation

Thanks to Saundra Huntley for graphic design and desktop publishing assistance. Thanks also to Troy Pongratz and Robert Schultzenberg for the inclined plane blueprints. Special thanks to Julie Miller Jones, 2003 Endowed Chair for Sciences, who gave us the seed money to start this project.

Version 1.0: printed August 2008 using Mindstorms education NXT Software version 1.0 and NXT Software 1.1 Special Upgrade

Version 1.1: printed November 2011 with Minnesota standards and engineering design process

ME Robots: Mechanical Engineering Basics is not directly associated with LEGO® Education. The trademarks (LEGO®, LEGO® Education, LEGO® MINDSTORMS NXT) are property of The LEGO® Group.

© 2008 St. Catherine University

TABLE OF CONTENTS

© 2008 St. Catherine University

INTRODUCTION AND KEY: HOW TO USE THIS BOOKLET

How does ME Robots relate to engineering?

Engineering is a discipline focused on creating products or systems that realistically meet human needs.

- Human needs can be foundational (shelter, food, transportation, defense), supplemental (for leisure, status, or special circumstances), or optimal (faster, cheaper, stronger, lighter).
- **Constraints** tie the solutions to reality because material or human resources are limited, time is critical, or money is scarce.
- The **disciplined process (engineering design process)** leverages existing technology, knowledge of how the world works (usually from science), and a logical reasoning system (usually mathematically based).

ME Robots introduces elementary-aged children to the three essential experience required to do well in engineering:

- **Exposure:** By having your children see and play with building materials and computer technology, they will be exposed to what engineers use and create.
- **Experience:** By having your children do the lessons, they gain experience in using the technology as it was intended.
- **Experiment:** By having your children engage in the mini-challenges posed in each lesson and the final challenge, they have time to experiment with ways to bend technology to their will and make their ideas a reality.

The **Engineering Design Process** is the way engineers combine creativity with scientific knowledge and observation, as well as mathematical quantification and reasoning. For elementary-age students, it is the way to help them move from random trial-and-error to systematic problem solving (See *Engineering Design Process*).

How does ME Robots relate to mechanical engineering?

Mechanical engineering is a branch of engineering that focuses on the design and control of devices that move, heat (or cool), or make other devices.

ME Robots introduces elementary-aged children to the foundations of mechanical engineering foundations:

- **Structures and materials:** Materials are what structures are made of. Structures hold things up, keep them contained, or keep things protected. They range in size from towers and car chassis to phone cases and heart implants.
- **Machines and mechanisms:** Mechanisms change one type of motion (such as rotary, oscillating) to another type. Machines allow us to be stronger or faster than we would be without them (e.g. wrench or wheels on a skateboard).

© 2008 St. Catherine University

- **Sensors and actuators:** Sensors sense things that happen to a device such as being touched, lit up, or moved a certain distance. Actuators do things such as move or roll (such as a motor or a wheel).
- **Computer control:** Computers use information provided by sensors. They then control the machines and mechanisms through actuators. Sometimes, they move the entire structure (e.g. an autonomous robot).

Engineering Design Process (for beginners)

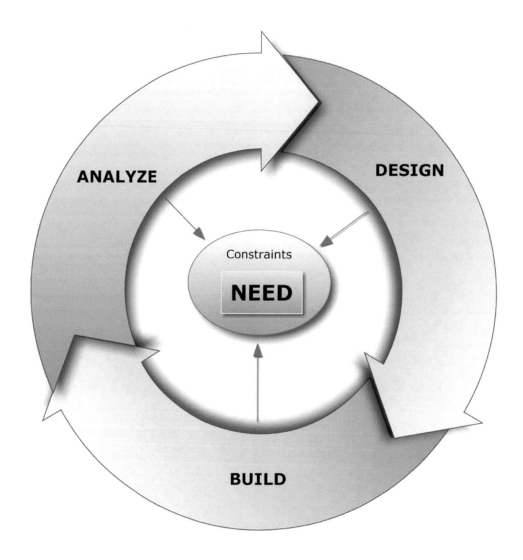

Need: Human need to be met
Constraints: Limitation of reality (limited time, money, material, labor)
Analyze: Figuring out why something happens
Design: Figuring out how something should be made
Build: Creating something to use, try out, or test

Developed at St. Catherine University's National Center for STEM Elementary Education

© 2008 St. Catherine University

Lesson Format

Each lesson's cover page summarizes the objectives of each lesson. It also indicates concepts introduced that relate to topics taught in school (*Academic Connections*) and technical terminology introduced (*Geek Speak*). The terms are defined in more detail in the *Geek Speak Glossary* in the Appendix.

The Pre-Planning section summarizes the materials and other requirements needed for the lesson. It also suggests the ideal way to organize groups. In your training, you will also learn about alternative ways you can group students depending on the equipment and materials that you have available.

Each lesson has Activities that are broken into numbered parts. The italicized items are notes to the instructor to highlight concepts that students might overlook.

 The gear icon indicates questions that can be posed to students for discussion.

Students may finish some lessons early. The section *If Students End Early* describes extra tasks students can do while waiting for others in the workshop to finish.

Each lesson ends with what students see in their Student Workbook.

The end of this booklet lists the science, mathematcs and engineering standards met by each lesson.

LEVEL 1 • CHALLENGE PROJECT
FOR ENGINEER-IN-TRAINING CERTIFICATION

Each level of ME Robots has its own challenge project. This allows students to see how their newfound knowledge and skills can be applied to a larger, meaningful project. Each of the lessons in a level introduces the concepts and builds the skills students need to solve the challenge project for Level 1's Engineer-in-Training certification.

The Challenge

Students will create a vertical motion machine that interacts with a horizontal motion machine.

Examples of vertical motion machines: elevators, lifts, escalators, Ferris wheels
Examples of horizontal motion machines: conveyor belts, cars, merry-go-rounds

Mechanical Concepts Covered in This Level

- Trusses
- Gears and pulleys
- Mechanical advantage and tradeoff of distance (speed) and force (power)
- Touch sensors

Programming Concepts Covered in This Level

- LEGO® NXT programming
- Outputs (Move and Motor commands)
- Conditionals (Touch Sensor command)
- *If time permits:* Repetition (infinite loops, counting loops, conditional loops)

© 2008 St. Catherine University

LEVEL 1 • LESSON 1
STRUCTURES, GEARS and PULLEYS

Objective

Participants will:
- Determine what makes a stable structure
- Build weight-bearing structures
- Make gear and pulley trains
- Describe characteristics of gears and pulleys

Academic Connections

- Math – geometry, ratios, diameter
- Science – gears, pulleys, mechanical advantage, inertia

Geek Speak (terms introduced—definitions in Geek Speak Glossary)

- Brick
- Gear
- Axle
- Bushing
- Gear Train
- Beam
- Connector
- Driver (also known as drive gear, driver gear, drive pulley, driver pulley, master)
- Follower (also known as follower gear, follower pulley, slave)

© 2008 St. Catherine University

Pre-Planning

Plan for 2 students per group

Materials
Each group will need:
- Minimum of 7 beams and 7 connectors
- The weighted brick or other weighted object (e.g., book, stapler)
- Minimum of 3 straight (flat) gears, 2 the same size
- Minimum of 2 axles
- Minimum of 4 bushings
- Minimum of 4 pulleys, 2 pairs that are different sizes
- Minimum of 2 rubber bands that can stretch over 2 pulleys and connect them

Or, the LEGO® Motorized Simple Machine kit

*Make sure each gear has one tooth colored on each side (Figure 1.1)

Student Activities

Activity 1 – LEGO® scavenger hunt
Materials needed for each group:
- LEGO® kits with different types of pieces

1. Look for different pieces in LEGO® kits: find familiar and new pieces.
2. Sketch 3 different pieces in workbook.

Activity 2 – Build a strong structure to hold a book
Materials needed for each group:
- 7 beams
- 7 connectors
- Something with weight (e.g., book, stapler, weighted brick)

1. Build a rectangle or square using 4-8 pieces (Figure 1.2).
   If students did not use connectors, give them the idea to try that.

How do the pieces get connected?
Beams are best connected with connectors.

2. Without dismantling the rectangle, build a separate triangle using 3-6 pieces (Figure 1.3).

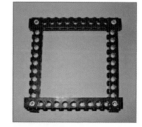

Figure 1.1

Figure 1.2

Figure 1.3

© 2008 St. Catherine University

3. Compare the strength of each by applying forces in different places with the structure in different orientations.

Is the square or the triangle stronger? Which is more stable?
Triangle.

4. Sketch structures in workbook.
Remind students that the sketches don't need to be exact reproductions of what they see. See examples in workbook.

How can you make the rectangle or square stronger?
Add axles or beams to brace two adjacent sides with a triangle (Figure 1.4). Details show how this could be constructed with LEGO® parts (Figure 1.4 a and b).

5. Build a structure to hold a certain weight 3" off the table.
Use either the weighted brick or some other object, such as a book.

Activity 3 – Introduction to gears

Materials needed for each group:
- 5 gears, 2 the same size, 3 of different sizes
- 3 axles
- 4 bushings
- 1 beam

1. Count how many teeth are on the gears, with each person in the group counting at least one gear. Record findings in workbook.
2. Find 2 gears that are the same size; put gears on axle through a beam so they interlock with each other (Figure 1.5 a and b). You can lock the gears and axles in place with bushings. This arrangement is called a gear train.
3. One student will hold the gear train so that the other can see it; line up the colored teeth.
4. Turn one gear (driver) to observe what happens to the other gear (follower).
5. Switch so partner can turn the gear; each student will turn the gear and each will record observations in workbook.
6. Share your observations.
Write the students' observations on board to share.

What do you observe?
The gears turn in opposite directions; the gears turn at the same speed.

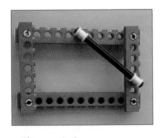

Figure 1.4

Figure 1.4a

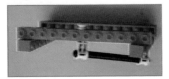

Figure 1.4b

Figure 1.5a

Figure 1.5b

© 2008 St. Catherine University

5

Activity 4 – Using gear train to increase or decrease follower speed

Materials needed for each group:
- Gear train constructed in Activity 3
- Remaining parts not used in gear train

1. Change the size of one gear and line up the colored teeth (Figure 1.6).
   Students need to know the number of teeth on each gear.
2. One student will turn the drive gear so partner can observe what happens to the follower gear.
3. Switch so partner can turn the gear; each student will turn the gear and each will observe.
   Have one student turn one gear around once while partner counts the number of times the other gear turns.
4. Write observations in workbook, noting directions gears turn and the number of turns the larger and smaller gears turn with respect to each other.

 What happens with gears that are the same size and different sizes?
If they are the same size, the follower goes the same speed as the driver. If the larger gear is the driver, the follower will turn faster than the driver. If the smaller gear is the driver, the follower will turn slower than the driver.
Actually, there is a mathematical relationship between the size of the gears and the speeds. If the driver has 8 teeth and the follower has 40 teeth, the driver must turn 5 times before the follower turns once. Thus, the follower is 5 times slower than the driver. The ratio of teeth tells us the relative speed of the gears.

 Try a different combination of gears; predict the relative speeds of driver and follower before you turn the drive gear.
Students should use ratios when predicting relative speeds. A demonstration of how to calculate ratios may help.

5. Add another gear to the gear train (Figure 1.7).
6. Sketch your gear train using arrows to indicate direction.

 How does the third gear turn?
It turns in the same direction as the driver. The speed of a follower depends on the ratio of the driver and the follower gear teeth. If the follower has the same number of teeth as the driver, it will have the same speed.

Activity 5 – Introduction to pulley systems

Materials needed for each group:
- 2 pulleys of the same size
- 1 beam
- 2 axles
- 4 bushings
- 2 rubber bands that can stretch over 2 pulleys and connect them

Figure 1.6

Figure 1.7

© 2008 St. Catherine University

1. Put 1 pulley on each axle then push the axle through a beam. The pulley that is turned is the driver; the other is the follower.
2. Connect the pulleys with a rubber band (Figure 1.8 a and b). Sketch the assembly in workbook.
3. Turn the driver once around; partner should count the number of times the follower turns.
4. While one student turns the driver, the partner should try to hold the follower pulley still—like applying the brakes (hold just the pulley, not the rubber band). Try doing this with the gear train as well. Write observations in workbook, noting the relative speed and direction of the pulleys.

What happens in each setup?
The pulley system "slips." The rubber band slips on the follower pulley when it is held in place, but the driver can still turn.
The gear system "locks." If the follower doesn't turn, the driver will not turn or the gears will dislodge. If the driver is prevented from turning, the motor attached to it may get damaged or "stripped."

When would it make sense to use a gear train? A pulley train?
A gear system is better for complete connection to the motor, but a pulley system can handle more variances. Pulleys are good if the motor sometimes starts and stops. The pulley wheel can keep turning (due to inertia) even if the motor stops temporarily. Wind-, water-, and animal-based systems often use pulley systems for this reason (e.g., windmills, water wheels, and an animal moving in a circle like the scene in the blacksmiths' shop in Pirates of the Caribbean).

Activity 6 – Use pulleys to reduce or increase speed

Materials needed for each group:
- 4 pulleys, 2 pairs of different sizes
- 1 beam
- 3 axles
- 4 bushings

1. Replace one pulley with a different sized pulley; turn one pulley and observe.
   Pulleys with different diameters will either reduce or increase speed. If the driver pulley is larger, the follower speed will be faster than the driver's speed. If it is smaller, the follower will be slower.
2. Add another pulley to the system. This can be done by adding one wheel on the same axle as an existing pulley (Figure 1.9).

What do you observe?
Pulleys still turn in the same direction. Depending on the ratios of the diameters, you can make the follower pulleys go much slower or faster than the driver. This greatly increases or decreases mechanical advantage of the system.

Figure 1.8a   Figure 1.8b

Figure 1.9

© 2008 St. Catherine University

WHAT STUDENTS SEE

LEVEL 1 • LESSON 1
ACTIVITIES 1 AND 2

How is the schematic the same as the photo?

How is it different?

Which is easier for you to draw?

Which parts are important to draw?

How much detail is needed?

Photos

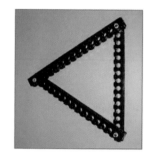

Schematics

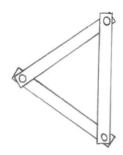

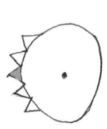

© 2008 St. Catherine University

What is the difference between the top view and the front view?

What detail are in the schematic?

What is the difference between the driver arrow and the follower arrow?

What changes if the driver arrow went counter-clockwise?

Top View

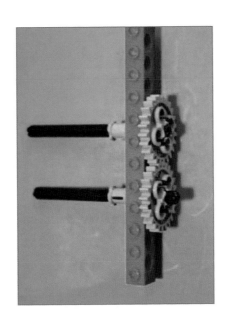

Front View

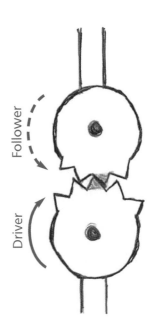

Try drawing pieces with pencil first.

Then use a pen to ink the "important parts."

Then use an eraser to clean off the pencil marks
(*That's how these schematics were drawn!*)

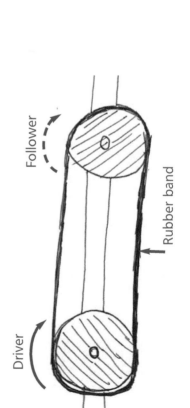

Two Pulley system

One pulley system

Follower

Driver

Rubber band

© 2008 St. Catherine University

LEVEL 1 • LESSON 2
SPEED vs. POWER

Objective
Participants will:
- Define speed and power
- Know the difference between speed and power
- Make changes in a gear or pulley system to increase either speed or power

Academic Connections
- Math – ratios
- Science – speed, work, energy, power, mechanical advantage

Geek Speak
- Motor
- Microprocessor brick (also known as intelligent brick, RCX, RCX box)
- Connection wires
- Wheels
- Plates
- Inclined plane
- High gear
- Low gear
- Speed
- Work
- Energy
- Power

Pre-Planning

Plan for 2-4 students per group

Materials
Each group will need:
- 1 Motor
- 1 Microprocessor brick

Other requirements
- Flat area for speed trials
- Ramps of 3 different heights (About 6", 9½" and 14½". See Appendix "Blueprints for Ramps")
- A way to measure distance: you can measure out a specific length that all groups will use, you can have them count tiles on the floor if it is tiled, or they can use their feet, rulers, etc.
- A way to measure time: you can use a second hand on a watch, clock, or a stop watch, or have students count seconds. For the latter, practice before the activity so the students count with the same beat
- A collection of different sized gears, pulleys, plates, bricks, beams, axles, connection wires and wheels so students can build their own vehicles
- Design a program for the motor to run (See Appendix "Simple Motor Program")
- Download Simple Motor Program to microprocessor

Student Activities

Activity 1 – Construct a vehicle to move on flat and inclined planes
Materials needed for each group:
- 1 motor
- 1 microprocessor brick
- A collection of different sized gears, pulleys, plates, bricks, beams, axles, connection wires and wheels so students can build their own vehicles

1. Build a vehicle using the same sized gear or pulley on the driver and follower. The follower or driver should be able to be changed easily. The microprocessor brick does not need to be built into the vehicle. It can be held in the student's hand and connected to the motor with a long connection wire (Figure 2.1 a, b and c).
2. Students complete the chart in their workbook, noting the gear/pulley sizes used.
3. Connect the microprocessor brick to the motor by attaching one end of a connecting wire to the motor and the other end to port A, B, or C on the microprocessor brick. Make sure the metal on the connector wire touches the metal on the motor.

Figure 2.1a

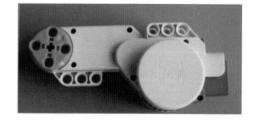

Figure 2.1b

Figure 2.1c

12

© 2008 St. Catherine University

4. Turn on microprocessor box by pressing the orange button.
   - Use the gray triangles to scroll through the files. A 3-sided box will highlight individual files. Highlight the program file: Run. Press the orange button to select.
   - Press the orange button to run the program.
   - Press the dark gray button to stop the program.
   - You can get back to the files list by clicking the dark gray button again. Click the button one more time to get back to the main menu.
   - To turn off the microprocessor, press the dark gray button under the orange button until you see a check mark. Then press the orange button.

5. Perform 3 trials of running the vehicle a certain distance on a straight, flat surface. Keep track of the time and distance in workbook (see appendix "What Students See"). Each person should have a chance to count the time; all in the group should record the time. Note any other observations (such as wheels spinning but vehicle not moving, vehicle tipping over) in workbook.
   If students can handle more math, they can calculate the speed by dividing the distance traveled by the time. If groups have their cars travel different distances, speed calculations allow comparison among car designs.

6. Run 3 trials on each ramp, starting at the bottom of each ramp (inclined plane). Note if the vehicle makes it to the top of the ramp or at what point the vehicle cannot go any further up the ramp. Note any other observations (such as wheels spinning but vehicle not moving, vehicle tipping over) in workbook.
   If students can handle more math, have them calculate the mechanical work done by the vehicle. This is done by weighing the vehicle or by estimating the weight. To estimate, you can create a chart of how much large parts (e.g., bricks, plates, wheels) weigh. Students would use this to add the weights together for the parts used in the car. Once the weight is determined, they multiply this by the vertical height the vehicle traveled. Work is defined by force divided by distance. In this case, the force exerted by the car is the weight of the car. The force is applied vertically, so only the height is needed. Students should not use the length of the ramp in this calculation. The work done by the vehicle is also known as the energy used by the vehicle. Since it is exerted in a specific period of time that students measured, students can also calculate the power of their car by dividing the work by the time. These calculations allow different vehicle designs to be compared to each other to determine which design is more powerful.

Are speed and power the same thing?
No. Speed is the distance a vehicle travels for a period of time. Power is the work (or energy) used for a period of time.

Activity 2 – Use gears to improve power output (force multiplier)

1. Change the size of one of the gears/pulleys so that the smaller one is on the driver. Note which sizes are used for the driver and the follower. Calculate the ratio and record in workbook.

2. Perform 3 trials of running the vehicle a certain distance on the flat surface. Record the times in workbook.
   If speeds were calculated before, have students calculate the speeds for this new design.

3. Perform 3 trials of running the vehicle up the ramps. Record how far the vehicle goes up the ramp and the time it takes.
   If work and power were calculated before, have students calculate them again for this new design.

© 2008 St. Catherine University

Activity 3 – Use gears to improve speed output (distance multiplier)

1. Change the size of one of the gears/pulleys so that the larger one is the driver. Note what size gear is on the motor and on the wheel. Calculate the ratio and record in workbook.
2. Run 3 trials of running the vehicle a certain distance on the flat surface. Record the times in workbook.

   If speeds were calculated before, have students calculate the speeds for this new design.
3. Perform 3 trials of running the vehicle up the ramps. Record how far the vehicle goes up the ramp and the time it takes.

   If work and power were calculated before, have students calculate them again for this new design.

 How can you give a machine more speed or power?
By changing any of the following:
- *Size of gear or pulley on the motor or wheels (which will change the gear or pulley ratios)*
- *Size of the wheels*
- *Weight of the vehicle*
- *Placement of wheels on vehicle*

 Which driver-to-follower set-up gave you the most speed?
When driver is larger than the follower, it will get the most speed. Running on a flat surface doesn't require a lot of work. This arrangement trades power (work in a second) for speed. This is the same as high gear on a bicycle or car.

 Which driver-to-follower set-up gave you the most power?
When driver is smaller than the follower, it will get the most power. Moving a car uphill takes a lot of work (think of walking up a hill versus walking on a flat surface), thus more power is needed. This arrangement is the same as low gear on a bicycle or car.

 How did you determine this relationship?
By timing on the flat (speed) and on the ramp (power).

If Students End Early

If students end an activity early or there is time at the end, have them start designing or building a machine that can lift a weight vertically, like an elevator.

© 2008 St. Catherine University

WHAT STUDENTS SEE

LEVEL 1 • LESSON 2
ACTIVITIES 1, 2 AND 3

Can you sketch the important parts of your vehicle?

Does drawing the vehicle from different views help document the design?

Remember to note the sizes of the gears and pulleys used for the driver and follower(s) when recording your vehicle's performance.

Make your own charts for Activities 2 and 3 on the next pages of the workbook.

Vehicle Performance	Flat Surface			Inclined Plane		
	Trial 1	Trial 2	Trial 3	Ramp 1 (lowest)	Ramp 2 (middle)	Ramp 3 (highest)
Driver Gear size ____ Follower Gear size ____ Gear ratio ____						
Distance travelled (remember units: Sally's feet, tiles, inches, etc)						
Time to travel (remember units)						
Speed = Distance / Time (remember units)						
(optional: Work done)	X	X	X			

© 2008 St. Catherine University

LEVEL 1 • LESSON 3
VERTICAL MOTION AND
INTRODUCTION TO PROGRAMMING

Objective
Participants will:
- Build a machine that will lift a weight, using knowledge from Lessons 1 and 2
- Learn different output programming commands
- Design a program to run a machine

Academic Connections
- Math – logical reasoning
- Computer Science – outputs

Geek Speak
- Tower
- Firmware
- Port
- Sensor
- Program
- Output

© 2008 St. Catherine University

Pre-Planning

Plan for 2-4 students per group

Materials
Each group will need:
- 1 Motor
- 1 Microprocessor brick

Other requirements
- A collection of different sized gears, pulleys, plates, bricks, beams, axles, connection wires and wheels so groups can build their own vertical machine
- Check that microprocessor bricks have batteries

Student Activities

Activity 1 – Build a machine with vertical motion
Materials needed for each group:
- 1 motor
- 1 microprocessor brick
- A collection of different sized gears, pulleys, plates, bricks, beams, axles, connection wires and wheels so students can build their own machines

1. Build a structure that will lift the LEGO® weight vertically.
2. Think of at least 3 actions for machine to do and record in notebook (e.g., move weight up, move weight down, spin, stop motion, pause motion).

Activity 2 – Introduction to the microprocessor brick
1. Locate the following ports and buttons on microprocessor brick (Figure 3.1):
   - Ports A, B, and C are for motors (Figure 3.2)
   - Ports 1, 2, 3 and 4 are for sensors (Figure 3.3)
   - Orange button to turn on microprocessor brick and select
   - Dark gray button to stop program and turn off the microprocessor
   - Trianglular buttons to scroll through menus

Figure 3.1

Figure 3.2

Figure 3.3

18

© 2008 St. Catherine University

2. These instructions are for the NXT microprocessor brick. The programs should already be downloaded:
   - Turn on microprocessor box by pressing the orange button.
   - Use the gray triangles to scroll through the files. A 3-sided box will highlight individual files. Highlight the program file to run. Press the orange button to select.
   - Press the orange button to run the program.
   - Press the dark gray button to stop the program.
   - You can get back to the files list by clicking the dark gray button again. Click the button one more time to get back to the main menu.
   - To turn off the microprocessor, press the dark gray button under the orange button until you see a check mark. Then press the orange button.

Activity 3 – Introduction to NXT programming

These instructions will guide you through setting up a program that will run a motor attached to Port A for 1 minute in a clockwise direction. Basically, you will create a new program, define a Move command and a Motor command, save the program and download it to the microprocessor brick. This program is used in Lesson 2.

1. Getting started
   - Open the NXT software application on the computer by clicking the icon (Figure 3.4).
   - On the NXT opening window, type in "Run" under "Start new program" (Figure 3.5).

2. Define Move command
   - Move your cursor over the Common icon (Figure 3.6).
   - Move your cursor over the Move icon (Figure 3.7). Click and drag this icon over the Start area.
   - With the Move icon selected, click on port A to indicate that you will be plugging the connecting wire into Port A on the microprocessor brick (Figure 3.8).
   - Click on the Up Arrow icon. This will have your motor run in a clockwise direction.
   - Set the Power slide to 100.
   - Select Seconds from the Duration box. Type in 60 to have the device move for 1 minute.

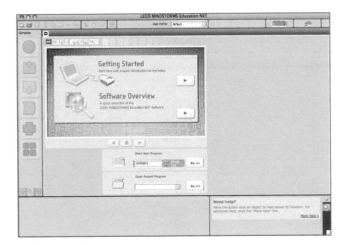

Figure 3.5

Figure 3.4

Figure 3.6

Figure 3.7

© 2008 St. Catherine University

3. Save and download program
- Select File from the top menu bar, then Save to save your program.
- Plug one end of the USB cable into your computer. Plug the other end into the NXT microprocessor brick.
- Click the Download icon. It is located in the lower left corner of the programming workspace area (Figure 3.9).
- When the program is finished downloading, you will hear a sound.
- Download this program to all of the NXT microprocessor bricks you will be using in Lesson 2. This program allows the NXT microprocessor to act as a battery pack for Lesson 2.

Activity 4 – Control the machine with a program

1. Write a program so that the machine will lift a weight, stop, then lower a weight.
2. Add other commands as time permits (such as play music).
3. Keep the machines assembled for the next lesson. Each group should remember the number of the microprocessor brick used so it can be used in the next lesson.

Figure 3.8

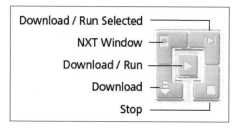

Figure 3.9

© 2008 St. Catherine University

LEVEL 1 • LESSON 4
PROGRAMMING with TOUCH SENSORS

Objective
Participants will:
- Learn to use the touch sensor
- Add a touch sensor to their vertical motion machine
- Program the touch sensor

Academic Connections
- Math – logical reasoning
- Computer Science – inputs, conditionals

Geek Speak
- Touch Sensor
- Conditional

© 2008 St. Catherine University

Pre-Planning

Same group arrangements as in Lesson 3

Materials
Each group will need:
- Machine built in Lesson 3
- 1 touch sensor
- 1 connection wire

Other requirements
- Check batteries in microprocessor brick
- Make sure students get same microprocessor bricks used in Lesson 3

Student Activities

Activity 1 – Build a machine with vertical motion
Materials needed for each group:
- Machine built in Lesson 3
- 1 touch sensor (Figure 4.1)
- 1 connection wire

1. Decide what the touch sensor should control. For example, when it is pressed, it could start or stop the motor.

What is a sensor?
A device that can sense something from its environment. This information is sent into the microprocessor brick and can be used to control a machine (the robot). Sensors are called "input" devices for this reason; they gather information from the real world and bring it into the computer.

What is a touch sensor?
A sensor that needs to be touched (pressed, released, or bumped) to be able to activate

2. Decide where the touch sensor should be located on the machine so it can be activated. Attach it.
3. Decide how the touch sensor will be activated: pressed, bumped or released. Pressed is the easiest to work with. Use the following sentence to help you decide activation needed:
   When the button on the sensor is ___ (pressed, bumped or released), I want the motor to ___ (start, stop).

Figure 4.1

© 2008 St. Catherine University

How does a touch sensor work? How it is activated?

A LEGO® touch sensor can be pressed, released or bumped. Bumping is the same as "clicking" (e.g., clicking the mouse button on a computer). A "bump" or a "click" is when the sensor is pressed then released.

4. Connect the touch sensor to either port 1, 2, 3 or 4 (Figure 4.2). The other end of the connecting wire connects to the back of the touch sensor (Figure 4.3).
   - To program the touch sensor, start the Mindstorms NXT software on your computer.
   - Move your cursor over the Sensor icon (Figure 4.4).
   - Click and drag the Touch Sensor icon to the programming workspace (Figure 4.5).
   - At the bottom of the screen, choose the action to activate when the touch sensor is used. Your choices are "Pressed", "Released" or "Bumped" (Figure 4.6).
   - Put the commands you want the sensor to activate directly after the Sensor icon.

   If the sensor will start the motor, the program should have some variation of the "On" command in the chain of commands. If it is supposed to stop the motor, the program should have some variation of the "Off" command in the chain of commands.

5. Test the program with the machine. Make changes as needed until it does what is desired.

Activity 2 – Control other operations

1. Create and run test programs with the following commands in the chain of commands instead of the "On" or "Off":
   - Sound
   - WaitBeep
   - Loop
2. Modify the test programs to determine how they differ from other commands that are slight variations from each other.

What happens? How does the input command (Sensor icon) differ from the output commands (Motor, Move, Sound, etc.)?

Its chain of commands are executed only if the condition is true. In this case, they are executed only if the touch sensor is pressed, released, or bumped.

If Students End Early

Design a program that will stop the motor when the touch sensor is pressed and starts the motor again when it is released.

Figure 4.2

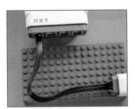

Figure 4.3

Figure 4.4

Figure 4.5

Figure 4.6

bar

© 2008 St. Catherine University

23

FINALÉ

Materials
- Machines made from Lesson 4

Other requirements
- Previous to the finalé, have the students decide how they are going to describe their machines, the process they went through to build and program their machines, and what their machines will do.
  Optional: Students could make posters for the finalé. The posters would include schematics of their machine design, their program, and pictures of the final product if you are able to print/develop them in time.

- Students will present their machines to the others in the group, and/or to parents and friends. This is a good way for them to show the results of their hard work and to explain to others what they did. This cements their understanding of both the design process and the concepts they have learned. It can be especially rewarding to the instructor when students use correct terminology rather than generic non-technical terms such as "doo-dad" or "thingy."

Presentation tips
- Set up the machines around the room. This way groups of guests can move from machine to machine. Students present to each group as they arrive with a standard presentation and answer questions the guests may have.

- If you want the students to be able to see each other's machines, divide each group so some students stay with the machine to explain it while the others move in a circuit through the room. Once the students moving around have seen all of the machines, have students switch roles.

GEEK SPEAK GLOSSARY

Axle – Rod that goes through the center of a wheel, *pulley* or *gear*. Connects the wheels to a structure and allows it to turn. For example, a car's axle connects the left wheel with the right one. In LEGO® kits, an axle is described by the number of cylinders it covers when you lay it on top of a *beam* or *plate* (e.g., a 2-length axle or a 10-length axle).

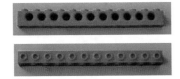

Beam – Construction element used in structures. For example, an I-beam is used in skyscrapers. In LEGO® kits, it is a long, usually black, piece that has holes through the side where *axles* or *connectors* can be placed and a row of short cylinders on the top. In LEGO® kits, a beam is described by the number of cylinders on the top.

Brick – Construction element used in structures. For example, red bricks are used in chimneys. In LEGO® kits, it is a thick piece that has short cylinders on the top which fit into the hollow opening on the bottom of a *beam*, brick, or *plate*. Described by the number of rows of cylinders by the number of columns of cylinders (e.g., 2x4 brick, 1x2 brick, 2x2 brick).

Bushing – Cylindrical piece that is placed on an *axle* to restrict sliding of parts on the axle. In LEGO® kits, bushings can be placed one way which locks an *axle* to a hole in a *plate*. When placed the other way, the *axle* can freely rotate above the *plate*.

Conditional – A programming operation that allows the *microprocessor* to "decide." If the condition were true, the operation would run one set of commands. If the command were false, it would run a different set of commands. For example, if the *touch sensor* were pressed, the conditional would turn the *motor* on. If the *touch sensor* were released, the program may do nothing or it may turn the *motor* off.

Connection Wires – See *Wire*.

Connector – A short tube-like element that can be pressed into holes in *beams* to connect them. In LEGO® kits, gray ones can spin in the holes; black ones tend not to spin.

Driver – The *gear* or *pulley* attached to the *motor*. It "drives" all other *gears* or *pulleys* connected to it (*followers*). Also known as *driver gear, driver pulley, master, master gear,* or *master pulley*.

Driver Gear – See *Driver*.

Driver Pulley – See *Driver*.

Download – The process of sending a *program* or data from one computer location to another. Usually referring to the process of transferring from a server or the Internet to a personal computer. In LEGO® kits, refers to process of transferring from the personal computer to the *microprocessor brick*. Opposite of *upload*.

Energy – The physical quantity that allows something to do *work*. It can take several forms: mechanical work, sound, light, electricity, magnetism, chemical, nuclear, or heat. Most common units of energy are ergs, calories, or Joules.

© 2008 St. Catherine University

Firmware – A *program* that runs on a particular *microprocessor*. It is like *software* in that it can be modified to do different tasks and is run by the *microprocessor*. However, it usually cannot be loaded onto other computers (such as your laptop), so it does not have much purpose outside of the particular *microprocessor* hardware. When you first start using the *microprocessor brick*, you must load the *firmware* into the *microprocessor*. This allows it to interpret the *software* programs you will then write and *upload* into the *microprocessor* to run your *motors*, use your *sensors*, or play music.

Follower – The *gear* or *pulley* that moves as a result of being connected to the *driver*. It is not attached to the *motor*. Also known as *follower gear, follower pulley, slave, slave gear* or *slave pulley*.

Follower Gear – See *Follower*.

Follower Pulley – See *Follower*.

Force – A push or a pull that makes an object change *speed*. Forces can make objects go faster (e.g., when you throw a ball, your hand applies a force to the ball to speed it up) or slower (e.g., when you catch a ball, your hand applies a force to the ball to slow it down). Typical units are pound-force (lbf) and Newton (N). The latter is the amount of force needed to accelerate a 1 kilogram mass 1 meter per second, every second.

Gear – An element that transfers the rotational *force* of a *motor* to another *gear* or device (like a *wheel*) through teeth or cogs. Because the teeth of *gears* mesh together, almost all of the force is transmitted from one gear to another, with little loss.

Gear Train – A series of *gears* that are arranged to efficiently transfer *work* done at one end of a *machine* to another end.

Hardware – The physical part of a computer including the integrated circuitry, screen, and buttons. As opposed to *software*.

High Gear – The gear arrangement where the *driver* gear is larger than the *follower*. When the diameter (or radius) of the *driver* is divided by the *follower's*, the *ratio* is a large (high) number. This arrangement gives the *machine* more distance for each turn of the *motor* (increases speed). However, it cannot do much work like go up a hill (decreases power).

Inclined Plane – One of the simple *machines* that can be made by placing a board diagonally on a high and low point, forming a ramp. Variations include a ramp for wheelchairs, stairs, a funnel, a screw (the screw threads are inclined planes), or an auger.

Inertia – An object's resistance to changing motion. This is usually paraphrased as "an object at rest stays at rest and an object in motion stays in motion unless an external force is applied." Thus, a block sliding on a table stops only because there is frictional force applied on it by the table and slight resistance from the air. If the block were moving in space, where there is no air and no friction, it would continue to move at the same speed indefinitely until it ran into something or something tried to stop it (both of these would be forces applied to the block).

Intelligent Brick – See *Microprocessor Brick*.

© 2008 St. Catherine University

Low Gear – The gear arrangement where the *driver gear* is smaller than the *follower*. When the diameter (or radius) of the *driver* is divided by the follower's, the *ratio* is a small (low) number. This arrangement gives the *machine* more *force* for each turn of the *motor* (increases power). However, it runs slower (decreases speed).

Machine – A device or series of devices that make *work* easier. Simple machines change the direction or magnitude of a force. The degree of change is described by the *mechanical advantage*. Complex machines are usually a combination of simple ones. For example, an old-fashioned wagon wheel is a simple machine because it consists of only a *wheel* and *axle*. A modern bicyle is a complex machine because the *wheel* and *axle* are connected by a chain to *gears*, which are in turn connected to the pedals—another form of *wheel* and *axle*. These simple machines combined together can give a *mechanical advantage* of 40-60x.

Master – See *Driver*.

Master Gear – See *Driver*.

Master Pulley – See *Driver*.

Mechanical Advantage – The *ratio* of the output *force* to the input *force*. If a *machine* is used, more *force* usually comes out than goes in. For example, with a car jack, you may put in your maximum *force* of 50 pounds, but the jack can lift a car which weighs 3000 pounds. The mechanical advantage of the jack would be 3000/50 or 60x.

Mechnical Work – The *energy* used to move an object a certain distance with a given *force*. For example, the *work* Wonder Woman does when stopping a runaway truck is the *force* she applies to the truck and the distance the truck travels from the time she applies the *force* to the time it actually comes to a stop. Typical units are Joules (Newton-meter), erg, or foot-pound.

Microprocessor – An electronic chip that contains a central processing unit (CPU). This is found in today's computer systems and allows the computer to be small enough to fit on a desk. The first computers were large, taking up entire rooms. Minicomputers of the 1970's were about the size of a dresser. The computer on your desk is a general computer that, with the right *software*, can perform a series of tasks from writing papers to playing games to interacting with the Internet. The microprocessor is the brain and the computer is the body.

Microprocessor Brick – In LEGO® kits, this large "brick" contains the *microprocessor* and the *power* (batteries) to run your robot/machine. Also known as *RCX, RCX box, intelligent brick,* or *NXT intelligent brick.*

Mindstorms – A LEGO® kit released in 1998 that combined electronic components (*motors, sensors*) with LEGO® structural pieces (*bricks, plates, beams*), also called the Robotics Invention System. The *microprocessor brick* that came with this kit is slightly different from the one that came in the next generation, LEGO® Mindstorms NXT. It contains the *microprocessor* chip which runs the *programs* students *download*, contains the batteries, connects to up to 3 *sensors* (through ports 1-3) and *powers* up to 3 *motors* (through ports A-C). Also known as Mindstorms 2.

Motor – In LEGO® kits, this is an electric motor which converts the electrical *energy* from the batteries into *mechanical work.* It is connected to the *microprocessor brick* using *connection wires* and can be controlled by the *program downloaded* into the *microprocessor.* Motors in general are used to turn an *axle* which may be connected to a *wheel* (e.g., in a car), *gears*, or *pulleys*.

NXT – The more recent ("next") version of LEGO® *Mindstorms*, released in 2006. Its *microprocessor brick* is slightly different from the one that came in the original *Mindstorms* kit. The *sensors* and *motors* from *Mindstorms* can be used with the *NXT brick* if converter cables are used.

Output – In computer programming, an output command sends a signal out of the computer to the real world through some sort of device. In LEGO® programming, examples would be commands that control output devices such as the Move or Motor commands.

Plate – A construction element used in structures for flat surfaces. For example, steel plates form the sides of a car, and aluminum plates are used for house siding. In LEGO® kits, it is a thin flat piece that has short cylinders on the top which fit into the hollow opening on the bottom of a *brick, beam* or plate. Described by the number of rows of cylinders by the number of columns of cylinders (e.g., a 1x1 plate, a 1x8 plate or a 2x8 plate).

Port – Place where the computer can interface with devices. In a computer, this could be a USB port where a jump drive can plug in or a video port where the monitor connects. In the LEGO® *microprocessor brick*, devices such as *motors* and *sensors* can be attached to the *microprocessor* by using connector cables to connect the device with the port.

Power – The rate at which *work* is performed. It is expressed in energy units per time. Common units are Watts (Joules/second), ergs/s, horsepower (hp), or foot-pounds per minute. Interestingly, James Watt, inventor of the steam engine, created the horsepower unit to explain the power of his new machine. One horsepower was defined as the ability to lift 550 pounds one foot in the air in one second. This is equal to about 746 watts. Here's a benchmark: A small VW Beetle from the 1970's had about 68 hp engine.

Program – Instructions for a computer. It is written in a language using a set of commands. For example, Java, C, and FORTRAN are commercially available programming languages. In LEGO® kits, a visual flow-chart language is used, but you could use one of the commercially available ones if you *download* the correct *firmware*.

Pulley – A *wheel* with a groove on the edge where a string, chain or belt can sit. Also called a sheave or block. Part of block and tackle or belt and pulley systems.

Ratio – The relationship one quantity has to another. For example, if one *wheel* has a radius of 10" and another has a radius of 2", the ratio is 10:2. When calculating *mechanical advantage*, the ratio is a fraction that indicates the advantage of using a *machine*. For example, if you exert 50 pounds on a car jack (*force* into *machine*) and lift up a 3000 lb car (*force* out of *machine*), the ratio of *force* out to *force* in is 3000:50 or 3000/50 or 60. The jack is said to have a *force* out-to-*force* in ratio of 60. Thus, if your little brother can only put 10 lb into the jack, he will lift a car that is 60x that *force* or 600 lb.

30

© 2008 St. Catherine University

RCX Box – Another name for the *Mindstorms* version of the *microprocessor brick*.

Sensor – A device that measures a physical quantity and converts it into something that can be read. For electronic sensors, the quantity is converted to an electrical signal that is read by the computer. For example, an electronic thermostat senses what the air temperature in a room is and sends a signal to the *microprocessor* to turn the furnace on or off.

Slave – See *Follower*.

Slave Gear – See *Follower*.

Slave Pulley – See *Follower*.

Software – *Programs* run by a computer's *hardware*. Examples include operating systems (Windows 2000/XP, Linux or MacOS) and applications (Microsoft Word, Excel, PrintMaster, FireFox, Norton AntiVirus).

Speed – The rate of motion, specifically the distance an object travels in a given period of time. Units are in distance divided by time. For example, meters per second (m/s), miles per hour (mph), or feet per minute (ft/min).

Straight Gear – A *gear* that is straight and flat, not curved or beveled. Also known as a flat *gear*.

Touch Sensor – A *sensor* that detects when it has been touched. In LEGO® kits, the *sensor* can be pressed, released, or bumped (pressed then released, creating a clicking sound).

Tower – In LEGO® *Mindstorms* kits, the device that connects to the computer and sends the *program* to the *microprocessor brick* using infrared light. In Mindstorms NXT, towers are not needed. The NXT *microprocessor brick* is attached directly to the computer.

Upload – The process of sending a *program* or data from one computer location to another. Usually referring to the process of transferring from a personal computer to a server or the Internet. In LEGO® kits, this is not done because the *microprocessor brick* does not transfer to the personal computer. Opposite of *download*.

Weighted Brick – In LEGO® kits, a *brick* that is particulary heavy because it contains a piece of metal.

Wheel – A circular device that spins on an *axle*. In LEGO® kits, wheel rims can be separated from the rubber treads to react differently with varied surfaces.

Wire – Thin, often flexible, metal rods that electrically connect two places. For example, electrical wires the in home connect the fuse box or circuit breaker box with the outlets. In LEGO® kits, *connnection wires* are used to connect the *microprocessor brick* with *motors*, *sensors*, etc.

Work – Normally referred to as *mechanical work*.

© 2008 St. Catherine University

SIMPLE MOTOR PROGRAM

These instructions will guide you through setting up a program that will run a motor attached to Port A for 1 minute in a clockwise direction. Basically, you will create a new program, define a Move command and a Motor command, save the program and download it to the microprocessor brick. This program is used in Lesson 2.

Getting started
1. Open the NXT software application on the computer by clicking the icon (Figure A.1).
2. On the NXT opening window, type in "Run" under "Start new program" (Figure A.2).

Define Move command
1. Move your cursor over the Common icon (Figure A.3).
2. Move your cursor over the Move icon (Figure A.4). Click and drag this icon over the Start area.
3. With the Move icon selected, click on port A to indicate that you will be plugging the connecting wire into Port A on the microprocessor brick (Figure A.5).
4. Click on the Up Arrow icon. This will have your motor run in a clockwise direction.
5. Set the Power slide to 100.
6. Select Seconds from the Duration box. Type in 60 to have the device move for 1 minute.

Figure A.1

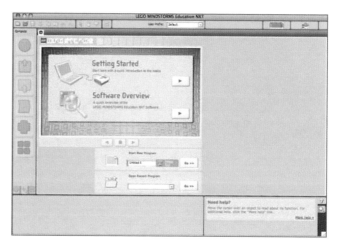

Figure A.2

Figure A.3

Figure A.4

Figure A.5

© 2008 St. Catherine University

Define Motor command

1. Move your cursor over the Action icon (Figure A.6). This will open a submenu of icons.
2. Move your cursor to the first icon in the submenu. It will be named "Motor." Be sure to use the first Motor icon. There is another icon that looks like a motor, which will be used in Level 2.
3. Click and drag the icon to the workspace and attach it to the end of the Move icon (Figure A.7).
4. With the Motor icon selected, click on Port A to indicate where the motor will be connected (Figure A.8).
5. Click on the Up Arrow icon to have the motor run in a clockwise direction.
6. Set the Power slide to 100.

Save and download program

1. Select File from the top menu bar, then Save to save your program.
2. Plug one end of the USB cable into your computer. Plug the other end into the NXT microprocessor brick.
3. Click the Download icon. It is located in the lower left corner of the programming workspace area (Figure A.9).
4. When the program is finished downloading, you will hear a sound.
5. Download this program to all of the NXT microprocessor bricks you will be using in Lesson 2. This program allows the NXT microprocessor to act as a battery pack for Lesson 2.

Figure A.7

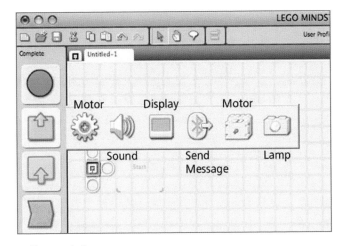

Figure A.6

Figure A.8

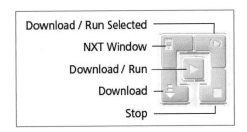

Figure A.9

INCLINED PLANE BLUEPRINT

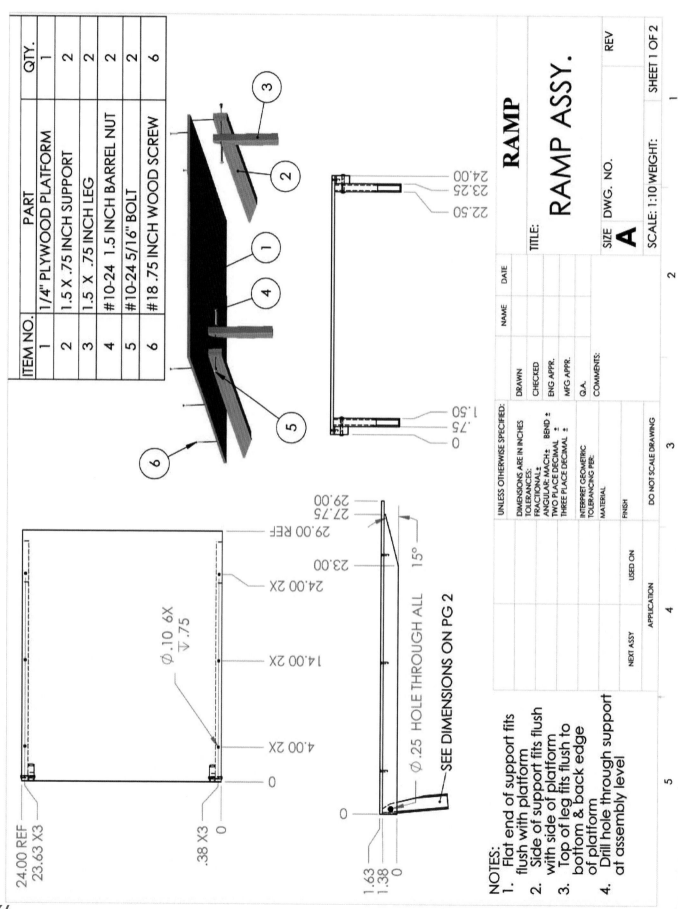

ITEM NO.	PART	QTY.
1	1/4" PLYWOOD PLATFORM	1
2	1.5 X .75 INCH SUPPORT	2
3	1.5 X .75 INCH LEG	2
4	#10-24 1.5 INCH BARREL NUT	2
5	#10-24 5/16" BOLT	2
6	#18 .75 INCH WOOD SCREW	6

RAMP

TITLE:

RAMP ASSY.

SIZE	DWG. NO.		REV
A			

SCALE: 1:10 WEIGHT: SHEET 1 OF 2

24.00
23.25
22.50

1.50
.75
0

UNLESS OTHERWISE SPECIFIED:		NAME	DATE
DIMENSIONS ARE IN INCHES	DRAWN		
TOLERANCES:	CHECKED		
FRACTIONAL±	ENG APPR.		
ANGULAR: MACH± BEND ±	MFG APPR.		
TWO PLACE DECIMAL ±	Q.A.		
THREE PLACE DECIMAL ±			
	COMMENTS:		
INTERPRET GEOMETRIC			
TOLERANCING PER:			
MATERIAL			
FINISH			
	DO NOT SCALE DRAWING		

NEXT ASSY   USED ON

APPLICATION

24.00 REF
23.63 X3

∅.10 6X
⩛ .75

24.00 2X

14.00 2X

4.00 2X

0

.38 X3
0

29.00
27.75
29.00 REF

23.00

15°

∅.25 HOLE THROUGH ALL

SEE DIMENSIONS ON PG 2

1.63
1.38
0

NOTES:
1. Flat end of support fits flush with platform
2. Side of support fits flush with side of platform
3. Top of leg fits flush to bottom & back edge of platform
4. Drill hole through support at assembly level

34

© 2008 St. Catherine University

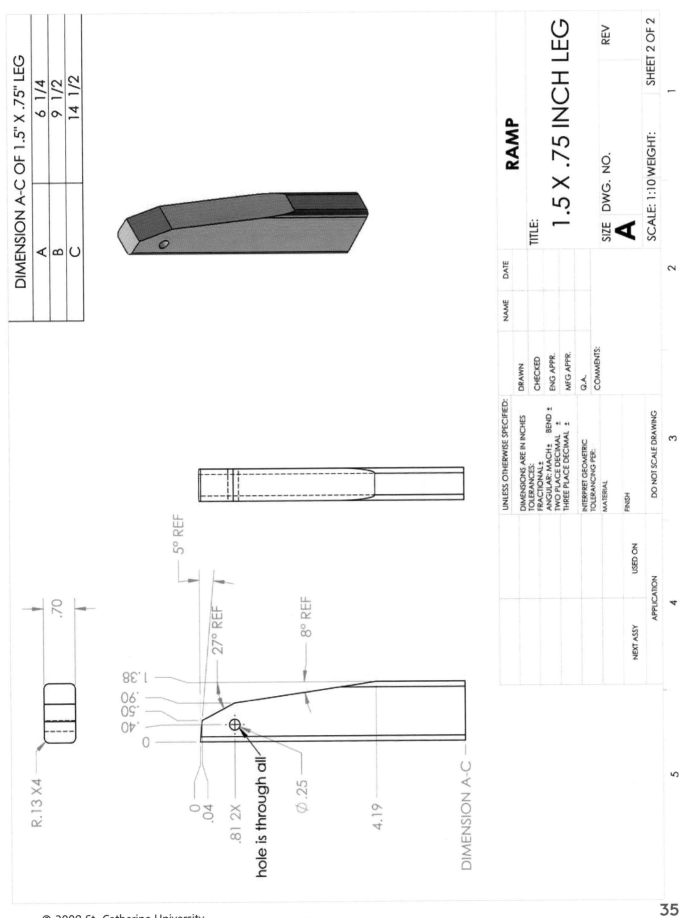

DIMENSION A-C OF 1.5" X .75" LEG

A	6 1/4
B	9 1/2
C	14 1/2

5° REF

27° REF

8° REF

.70

R.13 X4

1.38
.90
.50
.40
0

0
.04

.81 2X

hole is through all

Ø .25

4.19

DIMENSION A-C

RAMP

TITLE:

1.5 X .75 INCH LEG

SIZE DWG. NO.   REV

A

SCALE: 1:10 WEIGHT: SHEET 2 OF 2

UNLESS OTHERWISE SPECIFIED:

DIMENSIONS ARE IN INCHES
TOLERANCES:
FRACTIONAL±
ANGULAR: MACH±   BEND ±
TWO PLACE DECIMAL   ±
THREE PLACE DECIMAL ±

INTERPRET GEOMETRIC
TOLERANCING PER:

MATERIAL

FINISH

DO NOT SCALE DRAWING

	NAME	DATE
DRAWN		
CHECKED		
ENG APPR.		
MFG APPR.		
Q.A.		
COMMENTS:		

NEXT ASSY   USED ON

APPLICATION

5   4   3   2   1

© 2008 St. Catherine University

STANDARDS ALIGNMENT OF
ME ROBOTS: MECHANICAL ENGINEERING BASICS

Minnesota Mathematics Standards

Strand/Substrand/Standard	1	2	3	4
GRADE 3 **Strand** Number and Operation **Standard: Add and subtract multi-digit whole numbers; represent multiplication and division in various ways; solve real-world and mathematical problems using arithmetic.**	✔	✔		
Strand Geometry and Measurement **Standard: Use geometric attributes to describe and create shapes in various contexts.**	✔			
Standard: Collect, organize, display, and interpret data. Use labels and a variety of scales and units in displays.		✔		
GRADE 4 **Strand** Number and Operation **Standard: Demonstrate mastery of multiplication and division basic facts; multiply multi-digit numbers; solve real-world and mathematical problems using arithmetic.**	✔	✔		
Standard: Represent and compare fractions and decimals in real-world and mathematical situations; use place value to understand how decimals represent quantities.		✔		
Strand Data Analysis **Standard: Collect, organize, display and interpret data, including data collected over a period of time and data represented by fractions and decimals.**		✔		
GRADE 5 **Strand** Number and Operation **Standard: Divide multi-digit numbers; solve real-world and mathematical problems using arithmetic.**	✔	✔		
Strand Algebra **Standard: Recognize and represent patterns of change; use patterns, tables, graphs and rules to solve real-world and mathematical problems.**		✔		
GRADE 6 **Strand** Number and Operation **Standard: Understand the concept of ratio and its relationship to fractions and to the multiplication and division of whole numbers. Use ratios to solve real-world and mathematical problems.**	✔	✔		
Standard: Multiply and divide decimals, fractions and mixed numbers; solve real-world and mathematical problems using arithmetic with positive rational numbers.	✔	✔		
GRADE 7 **Strand** Number and Operation **Standard: Read, write, represent and compare positive and negative rational numbers, expressed as integers, fractions and decimals.**	✔	✔		
Standard: Calculate with positive and negative rational numbers, and rational numbers with whole number exponents, to solve real-world and mathematical problems.	✔	✔		
Strand Algebra **Standard: Recognize proportional relationships in real-world and mathematical situations; represent these and other relationships with tables, verbal descriptions, symbols and graphs; solve problems involving proportional relationships and explain results in the original context.**		✔		
GRADE 8 **Strand** Algebra **Standard: Recognize linear functions in real-world and mathematical situations; represent linear functions and other functions with tables, verbal descriptions, symbols and graphs; solve problems involving these functions and explain results in the original context.**		✔		

© 2008 St. Catherine University

Lesson

Strand/Substrand/Standard	1	2	3	4
GRADE 1 **Strand** The Nature of Science and Engineering **Substrand** Interactions Among Science, Technology, Engineering, Mathematics, and Society **Standard**: **Designed and natural systems exist in the world. These systems are made up of components that act within a system and interact with other systems.**	✔	✔		
GRADE 2 **Strand** The Nature of Science and Engineering **Substrand** The Practice of Science **Standard**: **Scientific inquiry is a set of interrelated processes incorporating multiple approaches that are used to pose questions about the natural world and investigate phenomena.**	✔	✔		
Substrand The Practice of Engineering **Standard**: **Engineering design is the process of identifying a problem and devising a product or process to solve the problem.**	✔	✔		
Strand Physical Science **Substrand** Motion **Standard**: **The motion of an object can be described by a change in its position over time.**	✔	✔		
Substrand Motion **Standard**: **The motion of an object can be changed by push or pull forces.**	✔	✔		
GRADE 4 **Strand** The Nature of Science and Engineering **Substrand** The Practice of Engineering **Standard**: **Engineering design is the process of identifying problems, developing multiple solutions, selecting the best possible solution, and building the product.**	✔	✔		
GRADE 5 **Strand** The Nature of Science and Engineering **Substrand** Interactions Among Science, Technology, Engineering, Mathematics, and Society **Standard**: **Tools and mathematics help scientists and engineers see more, measure more accurately, and do things that they could not otherwise accomplish.**		✔		
Strand Physical Science **Substrand** Motion **Standard**: **An object's motion is affected by forces and can be described by the object's speed and the direction it is moving.**	✔	✔		
GRADE 6 **Strand** The Nature of Science and Engineering **Substrand** The Practice of Engineering **Standard**: **Engineering design is the process of devising products, processes and systems that address a need, capitalize on an opportunity, or solve a specific problem.**		✔		
Strand The Nature of Science and Engineering **Substrand** Interactions Among Science, Technology, Engineering, and Mathematics and Society **Standard**: **Designed and natural systems exist in the world. These systems consist of components that act within the system and interact with other systems.**	✔	✔	✔	
Strand Physical Science **Substrand** Motion **Standard**: **The motion of an object can be described in terms of speed, direction and change of position.**		✔		
Standard: **Forces have magnitude and direction and affect the motion of objects.**	✔	✔		
GRADE 7 **Strand** The Nature of Science and Engineering **Substrand** Interactions Among Science, Technology, Engineering, Mathematics and Society **Standard**: **Current and emerging technologies have enabled humans to develop and use models to understand and communicate how natural and designed systems work and interact.**		✔		

© 2008 St. Catherine University

International Technology and Engineering Educators Association (iteea)

Strand/Substrand/Standard	1	2	3	4
GRADES K-2 **Standard 1:** Students will develop an understanding of the characteristics and scope of technology.	✔	✔	✔	
Standard 3: Students will develop an understanding of the relationships among technologies and the connections between technology and other fields of study.	✔	✔	✔	✔
Standard 8: Students will develop an understanding of the attributes of design.	✔	✔	✔	
Standard 9: Students will develop an understanding of engineering design.	✔	✔	✔	✔
Standard 10: Students will develop an understanding of the role of troubleshooting, research and development, invention and innovation, and experimentation in problem solving.	✔	✔	✔	✔
Standard 11: Students will develop the abilities to apply the design process.	✔	✔	✔	
Standard 12: Students will develop the abilities to use and maintain technological products and systems.	✔	✔	✔	✔
Standard 13: Students will develop the abilities to assess the impact of products and systems.	✔	✔		
GRADES 3-5 **Standard 1:** Students will develop an understanding of the characteristics and scope of technology.	✔	✔	✔	✔
Standard 2: Students will develop an understanding of the core concepts of technology.	✔	✔	✔	✔
Standard 3: Students will develop an understanding of the relationships among technologies and the connections between technology and other fields of study.	✔	✔	✔	
Standard 8: Students will develop an understanding of the attributes of design.	✔	✔	✔	✔
Standard 9: Students will develop an understanding of engineering design.	✔	✔	✔	✔
Standard 10: Students will develop an understanding of the role of troubleshooting, research and development, invention and innovation, and experimentation in problem solving.	✔	✔	✔	✔
Standard 11: Students will develop the abilities to apply the design process.	✔	✔	✔	✔
Standard 12: Students will develop the abilities to use and maintain technological products and systems.		✔	✔	
GRADES 6-8 **Standard 1:** Students will develop an understanding of the characteristics and scope of technology.	✔			
Standard 2: Students will develop an understanding of the core concepts of technology.	✔	✔	✔	✔
Standard 3: Students will develop an understanding of the relationships among technologies and the connections between technology and other fields of study.	✔	✔	✔	
Standard 8: Students will develop an understanding of the attributes of design.	✔	✔	✔	✔
Standard 9: Students will develop an understanding of engineering design.e	✔	✔	✔	✔
Standard 10: Students will develop an understanding of the role of troubleshooting, research and development, invention and innovation, and experimentation in problem solving.	✔	✔	✔	✔
Standard 11: Students will develop the abilities to apply the design process.	✔	✔	✔	✔
Standard 12: Students will develop the abilities to use and maintain technological products and systems.	✔	✔		

© 2008 St. Catherine University

30687104R00029

Made in the USA
Lexington, KY
12 March 2014